Purpose
In Your
Pain

Evangelist Stephanie Davenport

Published by Leading Through Living Community LLC

ISBN-13: 978-0692698815

ISBN-10: 0692698817

DEDICATION

This book is dedicated to my husband Alvin Davenport, whom I have seen experience pain in a myriad of ways, yet suffered with incredible grace and dignity: he experienced losing his both of his parents within a month's time. When one loses a parent, nothing can be said or done to make the pain go away. Only God can heal the pain, and it occurs over time. I love you Alvin.

To my aunt Elizabeth Berry, who has been in and out of the hospital and rehabilitation center for over a year. She has dealt with physical and spiritual pain. Losing something that or someone who has been a vital and active part of your life is not easy. I love you Aunt Elizabeth.

CONTENTS

ACKNOWLEDGMENTS

I want to give special thanks to my husband, Alvin Davenport, Jr., for his unconditional love and support. To my pastor, Dr. W. T. Edmondson for giving me his blessing and spiritual guidance. To Pastor Tifton Dobbs for encouraging me to keep writing and his words of encouragement. To Lynita Mitchell-Blackwell for inspiring me to follow my vision and to enlarge my territory. To Pastor Bertha Hodge for being a spiritual mentor and supporter. To Pastor Tracy Neal & Minister Connie Neal for compelling me to sharpen my skills in the word of God. To all my friends, family and supporters, this would not be possible if it had not been for you! Thank you!

PREFACE

Some types of pain cannot be communicated, no one can really know what you are dealing with because you do not understand it yourself. We asks ourselves answerless questions such as, "Why me?" Well, I always say, "Why not me?" If Jesus was persecuted, so too will we be. Suffering and pain is part of the ongoing journey of our lives. God has given us all we need to endure. We have to embrace and utilize the resources we have to endure. It is my hope that this book is one of them.

This book is for everyone who has experienced some type of pain. There are several types of pain you will read about in this book. I realize we all will experience pain, and sometimes it is so deep and bitter that we just want to stop living. But friend, we cannot stop living, loving and laughing. When we allow pain to take complete control of our lives - when we stop living - we are just existing. Jesus came that you may have life and have it more abundantly. That goes way beyond merely existing!

When we find ourselves in this place, we must be able to lean on God. When we are weak, He is strong. Pain comes in all types of forms, and no one can escape it, but we can learn how to be persistent during the process.

My prayer is that you will gain knowledge and spiritual guidance on how access the power within you to not only deal with the pain, but to understand the purpose for pain. Friend, without the pain, you would realize your full potential. Pain is required to birth what is in you. Just as women experience pain in birthing beautiful children, people must experience pain to birth extraordinary results.

God has given us what we need to endure. He will never leave us nor forsake us, even when we are going through. But we must go through: no gain, no pain!

INTRODUCTION

I have transitioned from one place in my life to another. I realize when looking back over my life, it was only the grace of God that brought me through: I would not even be able to understand how I am still standing if not for His mercy. There have been times in my life when I saw my physical body lying on the floor while looking down through my spiritual eyes. I was going through so much pain I just KNEW I would not be here the next moment, that surely I would die...

The mind is no help in this; it races constantly with so many thoughts until there is no rest that can be had, causing your physical body to collapse. We have to know when to surrender all to God. When the pain is too much to bear, we must surrender!

I have gone through several types of pain, and managed to endure. I am not resentful nor am I sorry. If I had not gone through those obstacles, I would not be the person I am today; and I surely would not have the relationship with God that I have now. I know without a shadow of a doubt it was the Lord who cared, and still cares for, me. He protected me and would not allow the devil to attack my soul - no matter how hard he tried (and he did try!).

I have learned to take this pain and utilize it to help me understand my purpose. It taught me to look at every situation differently, and to see the commonality of all those "different" situations: that all things work together for the good of them that love God and are called according to His purpose. Nothing goes on in the Kingdom without His consent.

One of my favorite songs is "This Place" by Tamela Mann because I never thought I would be in this place. What is "this place"? It is actually a time: one minute you may be up and things are going good and the next time, you may be going through and hurting in a place you never knew existed. People, even family, hurt you and you do not understand why or how you got to "this place". But I am thankful for Jesus who is always present in EVERY place! He knows how much we can take without breaking; and even when we are coming apart at the seams, Jesus is the great healer and is there for us always.

When we are hurting, Jesus says, "Come unto me, all ye that labor and are heavy laden and I will give you rest." When we are in pain, we need rest. Rest allows us to rejuvenate and get ready to get back on the road, to continue our journey. None said the road would be easy, and we do not know how long the pain will last... BUT just know something good will come out of the circumstance, whatever it may be.

If you never go through the pain, you will never know the outcome.

You are not alone during this process of pain. Do not give up - just look up because your father who art in heaven is making intercession for you. His eyes are on the sparrow and He watches over me and you.

We will come through as pure gold.

I pray this book will be an inspiration and will give you the tenacity to go through your pain with victory, cleaving to your purpose.

God bless you!

Evangelist Stephanie Davenport
A Healing For Your Soul Inc.

Part I:

Understanding Pain

CHAPTER 1
PURPOSE

In life there will always be pain, no matter how hard we try to avoid it, run from it, or even hide from it. But what we must do is embrace the pain, deal with the pain, and recover from the pain. The process always leads to what God has in store for your life. The pain causes the anointing to swell; if you never had any pain, how could you be an asset to those in need?

God allows us to go through different situations to make us better, to drawer us closer to him, to get our attention and to save us. When I think about every trial and test I have had to face, thy have made more humble, stronger, wiser, and greater in God.

What is the meaning of the word "PURPOSE". I could tell you what Webster says and I will, but this is what it means to me:

Purpose is the reason you have been placed on earth. It is the mandate that is on your life, it is the calling God has ordained you for. My purpose is not the same as yours. God has given us different gifts and talents, and He has anointed us for different things. I believe that we were destined to go through various types of pain so that God could use us for such a time as this -to fulfill the work He has called us to do. We would never even understand that we could go through unless God allowed us to be sifted and tempted by the enemy.

During the pain your faith is tested to see how much you will rely on God. People say, "God will never put more on you than you can bare", but consider this: if He never placed more on us than we could bare, how would we ever know how much more we could actually bare? I believe God puts more on us because He is building our spiritual muscles, pushing us out of our comfort zones, and showing us the inner and super natural strength through Him.

Webster says that PURPOSE is to do something, the effect of something, resolve, and intentions.

Did you ever ask yourself at some point in your life, "Why am I here?" "Why was I placed on this job?" "Why are some people in my life?"

If you think about it, it is for a purpose.

I asked myself the above questions for a long time when I worked in Corporate America. God showed me people who needed to ministered to, people who needed a change in their life, people I needed to encourage and pray for. After my time was up, God told me my season was up.

So many times we do not know why things happen, but God knows and He will reveal it to you in due time.

Purpose can take you places you have never been, it will allow you to meet people you have would have never met, and give you determination like never before.

If you don't know why you have been going through hell and high water, it is because God has need of you and He has a purpose for your life.

I never thought I would be preaching the word, or teaching about love, or counseling married couples; but God knew and He allowed me to go through a divorce, abusive relationships and remarry again. I have had to pray for people who did not like me, and even go visit people in the hospital who the doctor had given up for dead... and yet they live! I know God had a purpose for my life, but it was not until 2009 I began to really understand the calling on my life. I kept saying that after all this pain I have gone through something good has got to come out of it.

I am a testimony as to what God can do in your life. I wanted to give up, I thought about throwing in the towel so many times, but I would always pray and God would remove the thought. I was tired of relationships and friends who were not loyal. I got to a point felt that I had rather be alone and stay to myself... but that is not what God had planned for me.

What you have planned for your life may not be what God has planned, so be ready for change. God will change your plans to fulfill the purpose he has for your life. One that is victorious and successful, and overcomes all obstacles to His perfect will!

CHAPTER 2
PAIN IS PURPOSE

I never understood it until this very day that the pain I endured only pushed me further into my destiny. It is only when you are under pressure that you try to find your way out. The process of moving away from pain builds spiritual and emotional strength, fortifying your relationship with God.

Think of the pain and purpose the same way. There is a reason for every trial and every test. That reason is "PURPOSE". Ecclesiastes 3:1 says, "To everything there is a season, and a time to every purpose under the heaven."

Some people are not sure of what their purpose is, and if that is you, go to God in prayer and ask Him to show you.

5

Think about every situation you had to endure, compare them to one another, and note the similarities. Once you find the common thread, you will figure it out. Out of every trial, there is a reason, and something good will come out of it. Pain does not last always and neither does trouble. Genesis 50:20 tells us, "As for you, ye thought evil against me; but God meant it unto good, to bring to pass, as it is this day, to save much people alive."

Even when the devil tries you, God will turn it around for your good.

Embrace your pain, embrace your passion - it all will be used for your purpose!

CHAPTER 3
PERCEPTION OF PAIN

At the age of 44 I have experienced all types of pain, but I never realized until now that everyone does not perceive pain the same way. Some people pretend, compromise, hide and even deny the existence of pain so often that they do not know what pain is.

I noticed that men hardly ever show signs of pain unless it is the death of a very close family member or spouse. I noticed that women are generally more emotional and open about their pain, and appear to be more vulnerable to hurt than men. But even in making these observations, I realized that perception is dependent upon how good an actor a person happens to be; and that what is going on behind our "masks" will tell the real story.

Friend, pain is more than what you feel physically. It also includes what you feel mentally and spiritually. The heart and the mind connect. Once the mind comprehends the pain, the heart receives and then transfers it to the spirit. Once the spirit receives the "pain message", your physical being becomes weak. So it is your mindset that determines what your body feels. Your frame of mind determines your state of being: depression, oppression, loneliness, rejection, heaviness, angry and fear.

To stop these emotions dead in their tracks, we must face the pain, and deal with it mentally. This cuts off the circuit so the pain never makes it to the heart or the spirit. I know it sounds easier said than done, but believe me, you have the tools you need in your heart. When your heart is heavy, you must look to the rock that is higher than we are, which is Jesus. Jesus is our refuge and a present help in the time of trouble.

Only the power of the word of God will heal you from whatever pain you may be dealing with. Praying with God's word in your heart arms your to the teeth. God's word is powerful, quick and sharper than any two-edge sword. Using the word of God when praying allows us to talk to God, and remember and remind ourselves of the promise that He made to be with us always.

There is nothing too hard for God, and there is no pain that He cannot heal or disease He cannot cure. God's love for us is unconditional. Friend, pain is inevitable, but Jesus' love is forever! He promised He would never leave us nor forsake us. As long as we have Jesus, he will never allow us to deal with the pain alone.

Jesus said, "Lo, I am with thee. Jehovah Rahpa, which means the Lord that heals." (Isaiah 53:5) Jesus was wounded for transgression; he was bruised for our iniquities; the chastisement of our peace was upon him; and with his stripes we are healed.

No matter what pain you are dealing with, God can heal!

CHAPTER 4
WHAT DOES P.A.I.N. STAND FOR?

P stands for Perseverance
A stands for Anointing
I stands for Integrity
N stands for New

After we have suffered a while, God will establish, settle, and perfect you. When you have gone through this pain, after you have persevered, a fresh anointing will fall on you. This anointing comes from all you have endured. It built your integrity, your character, your strength, and your faith in God. Therefore, you are a new creature in Christ, you are no longer the same. You are stronger, wiser and better than before. "What does not break you will make you." Old things have passed away and now you are a new creature in

Christ. Press toward the mark of the high calling of God in Christ Jesus!

CHAPTER 5
THE PROCESS

Transition is not always good. The process is the actual change taking place in a definite manner. It is continuous action, moving forward. We do not always understand why things happen in our lives, but I know that everything happens for a reason.

When going through the process, pain is a part of that process. This word "PAIN" will always be a part of life. Pain is mental or emotional suffering or torment. It can be physical hurt, or distress, discomfort, agony, grief, harm, punishment, torture, or worry.

If the truth be told, we have never lived until we experienced some pain. There is a old saying that "We can never enjoy the sunshine, if there was never any rain". We would never have a testimony without a test.

There are some things we will have to go through while God is reconstructing our lives. It is like a blueprint that a builder has laid out for a new house. I remember when we were going through the building process for the new church. We prayed and fasted, the foundation was laid and the process began. There were many obstacles that came, but we looked at them as opportunities. Everything bad that could happen did happen to try to keep that church from being built, and it caused much pain. It caused disagreement, discord and discouragement; but can I tell you that we stood the test. We had to endure the pain of the process because it was necessary to achieve the ultimate goal - to build a new sanctuary. It showed our congregation that even in the midst of pain, God will always prevail. What He promised, He shall deliver.

The construction pain was a part of the completion process. The building was built, and it stands as the largest church in the West Point, Lanett, and Valley area, serving people from all over the area!

In our lives we will deal with adversity that will make us feel as if we are alone, embarrassed, and unimportant. These feelings can lead to frustration, discord, heaviness, confusion, disappointment... and doubt as to whether God is not with you. But know this: God is with you when you are going through the process.

We will face things in our lives that only we can go through so we may serve as witnesses to others. We do not always understand why we must be the vessel, but ultimately God allows things to happen so we may tell others that God, AND only God brought us out of the situation.

And here is a real doozy: is not always about us. When we go through pain, we would like to give in, give up, and even throw in the towel. But God is using us to reach other people. This entire life journey is about God getting the glory out of your life. It is about having faith in the almighty God.

The process is not to break you, but to make you. What does not kill you will only make you stronger. The outcome of the process is what is important. God would not allow the pain if there was not purpose!

Peter 5:10, "But the God of all grace, who hath called us unto his eternal glory by Christ Jesus, after that ye have suffered a while, make you perfect , establish, strengthen, settle you."

CHAPTER 6
TYPES OF PAIN

Life can overwhelm you to the core, causing your more primal instincts to kick in to protect you. That protect mode operates differently in every person, and it causes us to react in different ways.

Some people treat their pain as a private affair. Private pain is when you hide away from the world and pretend nothing is wrong, that the pain does not exist. Private pain causes us to be someone else to the world - to wear a mask to hide what we are truly feeling - and when we get home, we just sit alone to throw ashes and ask God WHY the thing that hurt us happened. We hide our hurt from family, co-workers, church members, and even our spouses. This pain is a secret and no one must know. People who process pain this way think, "What goes on inside me, or what I feel no one needs to know."

Then there are those who are more open about their pain. This is public pain. People who process pain publicly wear it all over their faces, and do not attempt to hold back their emotional turmoil. Public pain takes a toll on the body, wearing you down from the emotional exertion, and eventually it wears on the mind and the spirit as well. Some people call public pain a "pity party" because they perceive the openness of the pain as desiring attention from others. And sometimes the people we share our pain with cause us more harm and pain because they are not in our lives for good or to help us overcome our challenges.

Whether we process pain privately or publicly, pain is a very personal matter. Holding on to it too long causes it to grow into what is called personal pain. Personal pain lives in our hearts, and causes our hearts to so bad until we will let no one in. It becomes a strong hold that controls your entire being. This pain bring on depression and thoughts of suicide. It makes you feel helpless and out of control. To ensure personal pain does not take over your life, you must be able to identify its source - private or public - and cast the root of it (or all our cares) on the one who can heal the pain. His name is Jesus and he is a healer of all things.

Matthew 6:12-14 states, "And forgive us our debts, as we forgive our debtors, for if ye forgive men their trespasses, your Heavenly Father will also forgive you."

We often carry pain for a long time and this is when it becomes a stronghold, and unforgiveness takes root in the heart. We become bitter and the spirit of anger takes over.

If we want to be healed, we must let go and let God. We must forgive those who have hurt us, and we must forgive ourselves if we have hurt others.

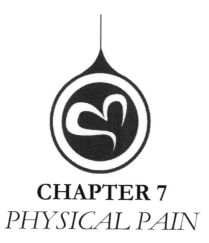

CHAPTER 7
PHYSICAL PAIN

Physical pain is one of the toughest to deal with because it is always present, front and center. However, when we understand that this pain is only temporary, then we can process it better. Our physically body does not understand the temporary nature of pain because the body - the flesh - feels that it is being crucified, tortured. Our bodies experience pain, some of which we have no control over, but our minds must be fortified with spiritual anointing to override that pain and remember it is only for a short time.

Jesus bore our pain and carried our sins. If anyone understands pain, it is Jesus! As he transition from spreading the gospel and healing the sick, he prepared to return to the Heavenly Father through the process of betrayal and crucifixion. Imagine the pain Jesus must have felt as he carried his own cross, was beaten, whipped, mocked, spat on, and then nailed to that same cross. Jesus bared much pain just for us, to forgive our sins. Friend, just as Jesus' pain prepared him to return to the Father, the pain you are experiencing is preparing you for another level in your life. It is a process to prepare you for greater that you could have ever envisioned for yourself! When you come through this, you will be like pure gold.

I remember the last time I had surgery, they cut me in the same place as a previous incision. The pain was so excruciating, it seemed unbearable. I have a high tolerance for physical pain, but I had to get prescription medication for this! It hurt to walk, bend and even sit up for long periods of time. But as time went by, the pain eventually went away. Although the pain was intense, it eventually went away - it was only for a short period of time. God's timing is not the same as our timing. A thousand years is a day to him. But our God is always on time, and He is always there when we are going through. He is our comforter, our healer, our peace, and our strength. When we are weak, He is strong.

We must understand that this physical body will soon be going to the ground and our spirit will go and be with the Lord. As you get older, you need to make sure you are taking good care of your physical body, and also feed your spiritual body on a daily basis with the word of God. Nurturing your spirit will help encourage yourself when you have no one else to call on. God sent His word to comfort us during those times.

No matter what pain we are facing in this life, Jesus can

heal us. Let His will be done in your life.

CHAPTER 8
PERSEVERING IN THE MIDST OF PAIN

At times we do not know how to persevere, how to endure. We want to push past and push through, but our flesh is weak. What we must remember in the weakness in our flesh is that our spirit is willing and strong! We must understand we are in the testing time, and if God is testing us, it means He knows we are strong enough to take it and not break.

I am reminded of the story of the children of Israel when they wanted to just give up and go back into slavery - SLAVERY! - simply because they did not want to deal with the uncertainty of what was in front of them. We cannot afford to have the same mentality as the children of Israel. We must hold on to our faith. No matter what is in front of us, we must depend on God and know that He is there with us in all ways.

Now, I have sympathy for the children of Israel: they were surrounded and seriously under attack. The enemy - Pharaoh - was behind them and the Red Sea in front of them. They could not go back and could not go forward. They were stuck... until they learned to depend on God. And God delivered them in an extraordinary way, slaying their enemies with the very sea that they perceived to be a hindrance.

Friend, we must depend on God even in the midst of adversity. Adversity will cause pain and sometimes the pain can be unbearable. Thank God for Jesus who is able to bear all our burdens and infirmities. First Peter 5:7 states, "Casting all your care upon him; for he care that for you, he knows how much you can bare."

Whatever present circumstances you are dealing with is not, and never will be, too hard for God. It may not feel good, look good or sound good, but just know that trouble does not last always. Find comfort in Psalms 30:5, "Weeping may endure for a night but joy comes in the morning."

When you are in a rut and you think you cannot make it another day, go ahead and tell your flesh to die so that your "spirit man" can take over. The Holy Spirit makes intercession for you to our Lord, who sits on the right hand of the Father. We must war in the spirit and not in the natural. When we are fighting in the natural, we tire easily;

but when we learn how to give the fight to Jesus - and leave it with Him - that he uses all of His power to win the war. Jesus does not tire, He never sleeps nor slumbers - he is omnipotent, all powerful, and always ready to act on our behalf. This is how He may promise in Matthew 11:28, "Come unto me, all ye that labor and are heavy laden, and I will give you rest."

Pain can be looked at as suffering, afflictions, and tribulation. We must endure hardness, as a good soldier of Jesus Christ. Suffering is the training ground for Christian maturity. It develops our patience and makes our final victory sweet. We must continue to endure and run the race with grace. Ecclesiastes 9:11 says, "I returned, and saw under the sun, that the race is not to the swift, nor the battle to the strong, neither yet bread to the wise, nor yet riches to men of understanding, nor yet favor to men of sill; by time and chance happeneth to them all." The race is won by those who love and depend on the Lord.

Here are the steps you need to persevere. You must

1. Change your mind set.
2. Change your position.
3. Focus on The Great Problem Solver (God) and not the problem.
4. Put on the whole armor of God.
5. Never let the enemy see you sweat.
6. Prepare a strategy.
7. Praise God unceasingly!

CHAPTER 9
THE PROCESS - PART 2

Let us look further at the process of pain. Now we know what the pain is, we have acknowledged that there is pain present, and now we must ACCEPT it.

There have been times in my life when I did not want to accept the pain, really see it for what it truly was. You may be in this phase of the process now. In order to deal with the pain, you must accept it by taking action... and this is the part that becomes tricky. You are hurting and want to move forward, but at the same time you want to stay put because you are not sure if more pain is around the corner. So know you must make the decision as to whether you are going to rusticate (stay and wither away) or rejuvenate.

And this is a HUGE decision because it will affect your destiny! If you never take any action, then you will delay the process or even prolong it.

Remember, pain is a process, and it takes time. That process will take as long as it takes - it can be relatively short or unbearably long, BUT when we are honest about what we are feeling and take action that is true to ourselves, then we can began the process to heal.

Friend, what decisions are you willing to make?
What will it take for you to move out of your comfort zone?

It is easy to be complacent while in the process and just go with the flow. But know that if you do that you are just settling for whatever comes your way instead being the Victor God wants you to be! If you settle for "whatever", what state of mind will you be in? Will you be vulnerable to the same type of pain again? Probably. Will you be strong enough to survive? Survive, yes; overcome and thrive - probably not. Why? Because you have not allowed your relationship with God to GROW. Remember, the process of pain is growth in your spiritual walk with the Lord. If you do not have a relationship with God when the wind of trouble comes, you can be easily be blown away.

While in the process you must be willing to move forward. As Paul stated in Philippians 3:13, "Brethren, I count not myself to have apprehended: but this one thing I do, forgetting those things which are behind and reaching fourth unto those things which are before, I press toward the mark for the prize of the high calling of God in Christ Jesus."

We can choose to accept and deal with it - "press toward the mark" or settle and become stagnant. Accept it and keep Jesus as your guide! He will never lead you astray. He is with you even in the process, but you must trust and rely on Him. Remember, it is not how you start the race, it is how you finish!

CHAPTER 10
PREPARATION

God will allow you to go through pain because He is preparing you for something greater.

Have you ever wondered why, when people are all around you, you still feel lonely? When last I experienced this feeling and asked God "Why?", He began to tell me that because of who I was and what He was doing in my life, it was time for preparation. Preparation for me was time to sharpen my skills, seek God's face, meditate on His word, and pray and fast. Although it felt as if I was all alone, I was in close relationship with the Lord as He readied me for the next phase of my life.

David is a wonderful Biblical example of preparation.

David was always in the field with the sheep, fighting off bears, lions and wolves .He was sharpening his skills and worshipping God many nights while he was alone in the field. He was sent there alone, without his brothers. When it was time to look for a successor for the next King, David was once again left alone in the field. He was looked over as not being qualified to rule, but when you have been chosen by God, it comes with favor. David was chosen as the next King because God had prepared him for greater than that field. When David stepped up to the plate to fight the Giant Goliath, he was alone. No one else was brave enough to do what David would do. God was with David, and gave him victory over his enemy. And friend I am here to tell you, God is with you, also.

God uses "alone time" to reveal many BIG things to us. In my own life, God began to show me that I needed to be separated from some people whom I had placed too much reliance. God wanted me to depend on HIM, not on man. God used separation to strengthen my relationship with him.

Separation is to disconnect or to go in a different direction. In life, separation is sometimes being a part from the people you love (and some of the people you think love you). Sometimes we love these people so much we are blind to their jealousy and envy of what God is doing in our lives. God will separate us to send us the message that He wants us to focus on Him and only Him.

God cannot also use isolation to send messages to us. To isolate is to set apart from others for a purpose. We cannot always see what God sees. He knows what is best for us because He knows our past, present and FUTURE.

If God isolates you from a person or a group, know that it is for a good reason - literally, it is to preserve your future victory.

Our future is predicated upon our present, and our present is determined by our current actions. Our actions are determined by our habits, and sometimes we tend to take on the habits of those we hang around. This can lead to the loss of our own identity, thereby compromising our relationship with God. When God created each of us, He created use to be unique, fearfully and wonderfully made: He does not want you to be like anyone else! God wants you to be the best you that you can be.

Our action are also determined by our spirit. Spirits transfer when you allow yourself to be influenced by people in your circle. To prevent such an occurrence, God will isolate you. It may be for a month, year, or eternity, but trust that it is all for preparation.

Last, God uses termination to strengthen his relationship with us. Termination simply means to bring something to an end. God does this to protect us, fortify our minds, bless our spirits, and bring us closer to Him. We have seen this when He prevents us from finding a job in an area we do not really belong in. We have seen him do this when He brings relationships to an end that should have ceased long ago.

God terminates certain situations that come about due to our faith becoming weak and our flesh becoming impatient. Those situations lead to us settling for anything. But friend, we were not made to settle for anything - we were made to be victorious in everything! So God will terminate you from that job to work for Him. He will terminate you from a marriage He did not bring together. He will terminate you from the wrong church - even if it happens to be during a time when you are not walking in His will.

God will call an end to those things in which He is not pleased.

We do not always understand the separation, isolation, or termination; but know that it is all preparing us for the promise God has for us.

1 Corinthians 2:9 But as it is written, Eye hath not seen, nor ear heard, neither have entered into the heart of man, the things which God hath prepared for them that love him.

CHAPTER 11

WHAT PAIN ARE YOU EXPERIENCING?

It is imperative that we acknowledge our true thoughts and feelings in all matters. Proverbs 23:7 states, "As a man thinks in his heart, so is he." There is emotional pain, spiritual pain, and physical pain. No matter the type of pain, we must be honest about what it is or we will not be able to get to the root of the issue.

Emotional pain is the most important component to understanding ourselves. When our hearts are heavy, the experience is a feeling of brokenness or a shattering of self. These feelings and emotions must be processed through to completion in order to promote a transformational view - of self, the world and one another.

Spiritual pain consists of the entirety of one's soulful experiences. These include fear, anxiety, grief, unrecognized guilt, unmet spiritual needs, and loss of control. We must be willing to submit our mind, body and soul to God without limitations. God will remove this pain from us, but it is a reminder of the things that endanger our salvation.

David experienced spiritual pain when his child was dying. Second Samuel 12:18 states, "And it came to pass on the seventh day, that the child died. And servants of David feared to tell him that the child was dead: for they said, Behold, while the child was yet alive, we spake unto him, and he would not hearken unto our voice: how will he then vex himself, if we tell him the child is dead." David experienced this pain because he had endangered his relationship with God instigating an unholy union with his officer's wife and orchestrating the man's death. God healed David from the pain, but only after he (David) confessed his sin.

Physical pain is the discomfort caused by disease, injury, or some other ailment in the body. Unrelieved physical pain can cause emotional or spiritual pain. When we are hurting in the natural, it begins to discourage the spirit. This is why it is important that we build our faith and know the promises of God. We must remind ourselves and encourage ourselves when faced with pain. We have to adjust to know that there is a healer and his name is Jesus!

The woman with the issue of blood had to have endured some pain. She bled for 12 years, but she had faith enough to go out to find some help for her hurt. When you are hurting, regardless of which pain it is, God is always there. Psalms 55:17 says, "Evening, morning and at noon, will I pray and cry aloud: and he shall hear my voice." Sometimes He is waiting on us to find Him, or just cry out to him.

CHAPTER 12
THE PAIN OF BETRAYAL

In life we will be betrayed, denied and persecuted. Jesus went through all of this when He became flesh and dwelt among us. We deal with betrayal in relationships, friendships, and even on our jobs. It causes us much pain.

Judas betrayed Jesus for three pieces of silver. Peter denied Jesus thrice before the cock crew. Jesus did nothing to them but be a friend and a leader who tried to lead them in the right direction. Jesus was persecuted, He was talked about, and accused of many false things. While we are living on earth, we will go through some of the same things.

We all have been hurt on occasions due to some form of

betrayal. What does this word mean? To betray another means to be unfaithful, to expose, to be disloyal, to disappoint the hopes or expectations of another. When considering this expansive definition, I am sure you, too, can say, "I have been betrayed." But how do you overcome it and forgive it?

We can overcome betrayal by guarding ourselves with the word of God.

The word of God will strengthen you in times of betrayal and pain. But first, we must identify the enemy, the person who has betrayed us. We must also be mindful of the words we speak and the actions we take so that we do not become like the person(s) who did us wrong. Next, we must ensure the people we have around us may be trusted. And last, but most importantly, we must watch and pray. Luke 18:1 tells us, "Men ought always to pray, and not faint."

The act of pray allows us to feel sympathy, empathy, forgiveness and love for the one(s) who disappointed us. James 1:19 says, "Wherefore, my beloved brethren, let every man be swift to hear, slow to speak, slow to wrath. We must love our enemy even more once we have knowledge of who it is." Although loving our enemy is difficult, it is imperative we do so. Matthew 5:44 says, "But I say unto you, 'Love your enemies, bless them that curse you, do good to them that hate you, and pray for them which despitefully use you and persecute you.' "

When we are in the midst of confronting betrayal, we feel lost and alone. We wonder, "Who can I really trust?" Psalms 56:11 has the answer: "In God have I put my trust:

I will not be afraid what man can do unto me." Proverbs 3:5 also states, "Trust in the Lord with all thine heart and lean not to your own understanding, but in all thy ways acknowledge him and he shall direct your path."

Confronting the betrayer

There will be times you want to confront the person who turned on you. But friend, let me tell you that you never have to confront that person because he or she will always reveal him/herself. Why? Because of guilt. Judas hung himself after he received the coins. Peter was crucified upside down and as a murderer. Everyone has a day where they will have to recompense for trouble. There is no need for you to take vengeance upon yourself; it will all be worked out in due time. Romans 12:19 states, "Dearly beloved, avenge not yourselves, but rather give place unto wrath: for it is written Vengeance is mine; I will repay, saith the Lord."

Betrayers will come to you in all forms: all genders, race, creeds and religions. Sometimes the ones closest to you are the ones you least expect yet will hurt you the most. And yet there is no need to be afraid or to live with your guard perpetually up: God reveals all things. Daniel 2:22 says, "He revealed the deep and secret things: he knoweth what is in the darkness and the light dwellers with him."

How do you work or live with people you do not trust?

But what if you are not able to remove yourself from a situation once you identify the betrayer? You must pray and complete your task. If the wrong-doer is a co-worker, continue to do your job. You cannot allow any room for personal feelings or emotions. Limit your interactions to what is required, and no more. Continue to perform to the best of your ability; people are always watching and you are always serving as a disciple of the Lord. Friend, I know it is hard and painful to work in a place where you feel you cannot trust anyone there, but until God moves you (through a new job, promotion, or task), then you must push through. Psalms 121 gives you motivation to do so, "I will lift up mine eyes unto the hills, from whence cometh my help. My help cometh from the Lord, which made heaven and earth."

But what if something happens that you feel you need to share with another? You cannot tell everyone your problems or confidential business. Some people do not understand what the word *confidentiality* means. But I know! It means what you tell me, is between you and me, and no one else. Unfortunately, some people forget that when they become upset with you. They feel justified betraying your confidence, sharing secrets in attempts to defame your character. In this journey I have learned to be silent and just tell Jesus when I am burdened or troubled. Jesus will not betray your confidence and you will not ever have to worry about hearing what you told Him again.

Love your enemies

We know that love bares all things. We have to love our enemies, even when we know they are the enemy. Romans 13:8 says, "Owe no man anything, but to love one another: for he that loveth another hath fulfilled the law." and Matthew 5:44 says, "But I say unto you, Love your enemies, bless them that curse you, and pray for them which despitefully use you."

God will give you the strength you need to overcome opposition in times of betrayal. When things seem too hard to bare, cast all your cares on God. His yoke is easy, and His burden is light.

CHAPTER 13
GROWING PAINS

Relationships are something you grow in. It takes two to love, two to hate. There is an old saying that, "There's a thin line between love and hate." This is so true. When you are in a relationship you find out so much about each other, and some surprises, too. I call this process Growing Pain really getting to know another person, and allowing yourself to be vulnerable enough to be known, can be painful.

We all have experienced pain in a relationship, whether it was in high school, college, friendship or marriage. When we discover information during the course of these relationships, pain can be amplified because we skip steps in the "getting to know you" phase that include

- Did you analyze the information?
- Was it accurate?
- Or did you assume?

In relationships we are so happy and excited to get to know a person, we ignore pertinent information about people's character. It is important that when we see certain behavior that we do not ignore it or try to reframe it into something more positive. We must accept, access, and adjust our thoughts and opinions based on what IS, not what we want to be. Being honest about how a person really is allows us to determine if he or she should be a part of our lives, and what part they should play in our lives - if any. If we determine that person must depart from us, we must move to separate immediately and with love. Some of us prolong the inevitable because we do not like confrontations or because we rather stick with "the devil we know". But this resistance to change creates frustration, which then leads to anger, and eventually we become bitter.

Growing pains are a natural part of every relationship and continue to occur as long as you are in relationship with others. Learning to deal with the issue at hand, no matter what it is, is the key to addressing growing pains. You must be able to say when enough is enough. There are some things in life you do not have to deal with, and some people you do not have to have in your life - regardless of the relationship you used to have. When people hurt you and take you for granted in a relationship, you must confront it head on - and make a decision as to when it is time to end it.

I know what I am saying is hard. When you have been

friends since high school, but the person continues to hurt you, you have a decision to make - are you really going to continue to tolerate that? Fifty years of marriage and your spouse continues to commit adultery - are you really going to continue to put her mind, heart, and soul through that?

If you decide to end the relationship, forgive the person. I cannot say "forgive" enough! Also, mentally be thankful that the person is gone and that you no longer have to grow with them. You are now ready to grow without them. What you decide will determine your destiny and also determine you tomorrow.

CHAPTER 14
GROWING WITH GOD

When you grow in God, you will go through pain. Some of your friends will not receive you because they are not where you are in developing self. Some will assume you have placed yourself above others. They do not understand that you have placed God above all else, and your focus is now on being available, authentic, successful, anointed, affluent and accessible to God's will.

I did not understand some of the pain I had to endure when I was younger, and it seemed that the pain became worse when I began to live for the Lord. People I thought loved me, left me. Friends that I trusted betrayed me. It seemed like the closer I got to God, the lonelier the walk became.

When you are growing in God, expect the pain to come. Look at how Jesus was rejected in his own town. And consider Paul who began building churches and called himself a slave for Christ - yet he experienced great pain.

Friend, do not be discouraged, even when you are going through. God will always send you someone for a season to encourage, teach and help you as you grow in Him, through Him and with Him. He always has a ram in bush, just as he did with Abraham.

This journey is not easy, and there will be "wilderness times", but this journey is preparing you for purpose. You will never know your purpose until you experience pain. The pain is what helps you become the true person you were meant to be and it births your talents and gifts to help achieve God's objectives. This process builds strength and character, and you will be able to handle situations some people would lose their minds even thinking about - but not you.

Philippians 3:7-10 KJV, "But what things were gain to me, those I counted loss for Christ. Yea doubtless, and I count all things but loss for the excellency of the knowledge of Christ Jesus my Lord: for whom I have suffered the loss of all things, and do count them but dung, that I may win Christ, And be found in him, not having mine own righteousness, which is of the law, but that which is through the faith of Christ, the righteousness which is of God by faith: That I may know him, and the power of his resurrection, and the fellowship of his sufferings, being made conformable unto his death".

CHAPTER 15
FAMILY HURT

You should be close to your family, and they should be your backbone when you have no one else. Family should be there to love, support, and encourage you in any situation. You will agree and disagree with your family, but those disagreements should never get to the point of hating one another.

When family members do things to hurt one another, this can cause serious pain, discord, confusion, and absence from the fold. The love bond should always be strong in the family, strong enough to counter these painful instances. You and your family carry the same blood, same last name, and a legacy that your mother, father, and fore-parents created for you to enjoy.

It really hurts to see family members not getting along and arguing over unnecessary things. It hurts to hear mean words and regret always follows because once those words come forth, they cannot be taken back and are hard to forget. People may not show it, or even say it, but words really pack a punch, and create deep wounds that are hard to mend. But when we have the love of God on the inside, we must forgive and show love at all times - even when we are hurting.

When we are experiencing family hurt, we must always forgive, and treat people the way we want to be treated - regardless as to what is going on. We must try to settle the dispute or disagreement, and even if we are not are not person in the wrong, sometimes we have to be the bigger person and take the blame for someone else's wrong.

Friend, why can we not just get along and love one another? I have seen so much family hurt in the last two years, it is almost unreal. It made me wonder more than a few times how one can say he loves Jesus whom he has never seen, yet hate his sister or brother who he sees every day!

Sometimes you have to disagree to agree. Sometimes you have to give each other space, but never allow anything or anyone to come between you or tamper with the love you have for each other.

People are dying every day and yet we cannot come together and love. God loved us so much He gave His only son so we may have a right to the tree of life. Instead of obeying His commandments to obey Him and love one another, we are doing the opposite. If you do not love and have no love in your heart for anyone else, then you are not living according to God's word.

Jesus said, "I came that you may have life and have it more abundantly". If you say you have Jesus on the inside, but you have no love in your heart, you have no understanding of Jesus or His love.

Find a way to resolve any family issues. If you cannot agree, love from a distance and be polite towards one another when in each other's presence.

1st Corinthians 13:4-8 KJV gives the blueprint for family love [charity], "Charity suffereth long, and is kind; charity envieth not; charity vaunteth not itself, is not puffed up, Doth not behave itself unseemly, seeketh not her own, is not easily provoked, thinketh no evil; Rejoiceth not in iniquity, but rejoiceth in the truth; Beareth all things, believeth all things, hopeth all things, endureth all things. Charity never faileth: but whether there be prophecies, they shall fail; whether there be tongues, they shall cease; whether there be knowledge, it shall vanish away."

CHAPTER 16
CHURCH HURT

I have been told by several people that there is no hurt like Church Hurt. Church hurt includes many things, such as a bad relationship between you and the pastor or the pastor's wife; or being looked over because you are gifted and anointed, and some people can be intimidated by it. Church hurt comes from the people of God hurting other believers in Christ.

The first thing you must do to overcome church hurt is by repentance. You must repent of your sins, and forgive those who have hurt or wronged you in any way. If possible, go to the person and ask for forgiveness. If they choose not to accept your humble apology, know you have done your part and move on. Close that chapter in life and move to the next. Paul says in Philippians 3:13-14, "Brethren, I count not myself to have apprehended: but this one thing I do, forgetting those things which are behind, and reaching forth unto those things which are before, I press toward the mark for the prize of the high calling of God in Christ Jesus."

The second step in being healed from church hurt is to dispose of any tangible gifts or intangible gifts that came with conditions. You must get rid of any memories or things that remind you of the past. These things keep you in bondage and prevent you from moving forward. You must put God first in your life and everything else must take a back seat. "You shall have no other Gods," Deuteronomy 28:36 KJV.

The last and most important thing you must do to be freed from church hurt is to focus on the love of God. Love covers a multitude of sin. You must realize that God is love and if you belong to Him, you also have to love everyone. Show love to those who have hurt you and those who have used you. When you can love in spite of that mistreatment, you have the assurance that greater is He that is in you than he that is in the world.

CHAPTER 17
WOUNDED ON THE JOB

Pain can come from any source. It is not always related to church, family or friends. You can be wounded on the job and this can be devastating. I have seen people who worked for several years for the same company, but were in so much pain. Why were they in pain, where did this pain come from? When I think about the world today and our relationships to with our employers, I think the source of work place pain is lack of leadership.

It seems that people do not care about work ethic (or lack thereof), team work or willingness to help, or gender or any other type of equality. It just seems that people want to be left alone, do enough to get a paycheck and go home. They do not want to be involved in any skirmish or situation that may make waves. They want to be politically correct and stay in their lanes. That type of disconnection requires a callousness of soul that creates pain. Friend, if you work for an organization like this, start looking for the closest exit and get out of there as soon as possible. Run like your life depends on it - because it does! Your spirit is taking a beating that will cause you pain for years to come.

I learned this the hard way. After working for a company for 14 years I saw the callousness in action, and saw how cold-hearted it made some people. I learned that no matter how hard you worked, how much you helped, how much you gave; that if you were not in the right circle and stayed in your lane, then you would never grow with the company. You had to play the game of being a "ride along". You could never voice your opinion because the boss would oppose it every time because he felt your opinions made him powerless and appear incompetent. That could not have been further from the truth. There were many other instances of pain in that workplace that included struggles over control, being passed over for promotion, overly critical evaluations, and being forced to report incompetent supervisors.

Friend, know that God is with you always, and in all ways, as you go through this pain. This pain happens because the people in your organization see the leader in you - with or without the title - and it angers and frightens them. When you show people you are your own person, and your peers look to you as a leader even without the title, then there will be a battle. Those you are battling against do not understand the majesty of the Most High. They do not understand how you can work in that company and be a leader without a title. They do not understand that when God made your name great you did not need man's title. They do not realize that you know in your heart that you can be who you are and still be great on the job - without their politics, "ride alongs" or other games. When you know who you are in God and who's you are, God will promote you. Psalm 75:6-8 KJV "For promotion cometh neither from the east, nor from the west, nor from the south. But God is the judge: he putteth down one, and setteth up another."

Pray before you go to work and while you are working. Work hard for the sake of glorifying God's name, and stay focused on His pleasure - He will not let you down. Psalm 146:3 KJV states, "Put not your trust in princes, nor in the son of man, in whom there is no help."

Friend, I was in a lot of pain when I left my last position. It began to make me bitter and I had to pray because I knew the enemy was really trying me. He had come to sift me and to take me out, but I knew God had a plan for my life. I am here to tell you that every day there will be struggles, but there are some things you can do to guard yourself from wounds on the job.

1. Maintain a professional distance - be cordial, but remember that co-workers are not friends.
2. Pay attention to the environment and pray unceasingly.
3. Be ready to move when it is time, and be wise in your affiliations.
4. Speak positively and avoid negative people and their gossip.

5. Know your duties and resources to do a great job.
6. Obtain a thorough understanding of company policy and procedure.
7. Maintain a list of important numbers, such as human resources, and local, state and/or federal agencies that govern your industry and company.

Even when you follow the above steps, you can still be wounded on the job, but you can recover from it. When you were little and fell off your bicycle, your mom or dad would say, "Get up and try again." That was great advice that applies here - getting up and trying again helps to shape you and make you better for the next position God has in store for you. It gives you power to try it again. There is a higher power behind you, and when the pain is too much to bear, God will make His face plain to pick you up and mend the brokenness in your heart.

Wounded in Your Own Business

Business partnerships can be a source of great joy and great pain. When the partnership is going well, you could not imagine doing business any other way than with your friend, buddy, and pal. But when things are falling apart, you cannot wait to separate from that person so you can run the business the way you envision - without interference. Friend, when business partners will not do right, God will release you and allow you to start your own enterprise without one. The pain God allows you to endure within the bad partnership is to teach you that 1) some people are not meant to be in your life and 2) you can and will enjoy success in the next venture without a partner. Running a successful business can be scary and challenging - it is one of the reasons we go into business with others, to share the risks and have built-in help. But choices made in fear and anxiety have consequences - and those consequences usually lead to Entrepreneurial pain.

Just as working for someone else can cause stress, so too does being in business with the wrong person. Some ventures give us migraines, high blood pressure, and stress us so badly that we have no peace at home or in church. Friend, go to work for God. Allow Him to remove this turmoil from you. When you see things coming apart at the seams, do not repair it - separate the parts and get about your Father's business!

According to Romans 5:1-6, God gives you benefits that the job cannot:

1. Faith
2. Peace
3. Position
4. Perseverance
5. Grace
6. Holy Ghost

I can tell you that when you put God first in your life, He will always lead you the right way. Our ways are not like His, but His way is the right way. His timing is not like ours, but He is always on time.

When you began to work for God, He will give you the desires of your heart. He will place you on a new job or in a new venture that will appreciate you and give you your time back.

"Seek ye kingdom first and his righteousness and all these things shall be added unto you."

CHAPTER 18
ROAD TO RECOVERY

We know that the wounds from all these types of pain can be very hurtful and deep, but we must focus on the process of healing these wounds from current circumstance and the past. Identifying exactly where the wound is, what caused the wound and why it hurts so bad is how we get on the road to recovery.

Often we ask questions like "why me", "why does it hurt so"; but the question should be "why not you"? If you never got a wound, you would never know how to heal, or the feeling of being hurt. It is good to be wounded, it is good to get the experience so you will know what to expect and what not to do. Wounds are pain, hurt feelings, injury to the body, disruption to character, life lessons, and corrections in attitude. Recovering from them involves

1. Taking ownership in the part you played in being hurt (remember, it takes two to tango!).
2. Reconciling with the other party(ies) and forgiving that person (or those persons) and yourself.
3. Leaving the past in the past. Eyes front!
4. Taking positive steps to build new relationships.

You cannot blame one person for everything. You must be able to identify things you did or did not do, or things that could have been done to make things better. So many times we want to do nothing and wait on others to come and fix our mistakes, but it takes everyone in the relationship to do something. You will never recover if nothing is done, and it must be done right. Just as a house must be built on solid foundation to prevent future problems, so too must you build your recovery upon earnest and humble efforts of reconciliation. You do not have to carry this wound around, open and bleeding. You can begin the process of healing immediately - it all begins with YOU.

How long will you let it linger? You cannot allow pride to get in the way of the recovery. If you want to be healed, you must act quickly.

I am reminded of this story of the man who sat by the pool, and at a certain time of the year the angel would come and stir up the water. Those who got in would be healed of all their infinities. This man sat at the pool for 38 years, and when Jesus showed up and asked him if he wanted to be healed, he had an excuse. (Many of us are making excuses instead of saying, "I want to be healed".) This man told Jesus that every time he got ready to get in the pool, someone jumped in before him. Jesus again asked the man if he wanted to be healed. Eventually the man answered yes, and you know the rest of the story.

So now I ask you - do you want to be healed? Your answer will dictate your destiny.

Part II:

Prayers for Pain

Prayer for Purpose

O gracious and eternal God, Savior, Jehovah, Elohim, you are all I need and I thank you for never leaving me nor forsaking me. Lord, please forgive me for being impatient, doubtful, and sometimes worried. I know you have my best interest at heart. I know you are always with me.

Lord, continue to show me the path you have for me. Lord, guide me into my purpose, show me what it is so I can fulfill it.

Lord, when I am in pain please continue to mend my heart when it is heavy, strengthen me when I a weak, build me up when I am down. When life seems to take a turn, Lord hold me and guide me to the path of righteousness.

Lord, I thank you for all you have done, and for every trial and test. Lord, you have blessed me in so many ways. I just want to say thank you.

Hallelujah. Amen!

Prayer of Faith

When you have no one to trust, have faith in God. I took that leap of faith and it changed my whole life! Once you take that leap of faith, pray with faith and believe that whatever you ask, you shall receive. Mark 11:22 tells us, "And Jesus answering saith unto them, 'Have faith in God. For verily I say unto you, That whosoever shall say unto this mountain, Be thou removed, and be thou cast into the sea; and shall not doubt in his heart, but shall believe that those things which he saith shall come to pass; he shall have whatsoever he saith. Therefore I say unto you, What things so ever ye desire, when ye pray, believe that ye receive them, and ye shall have them.' "

When you feel unsure or insecure, pray this prayer of faith:

Heavenly father, I thank you that the Just shall live by faith. When heaven and earth shall pass away, your word will remain. I thank you that you are a just and faithful God. Faithful and just to forgive us from all of our sins and unrighteousness, and throw them into the sea of forgetfulness and remember them no more.

Lord, I love you and you know me better than I know myself. Your word is a lamp unto my feet and light unto my path. I am leaning and depending on you, Lord. I know now that it is impossible to please you without faith. For we walk by faith and not by sight. Faith is the substance of things hope for and the evidence of things not seen. Lord, I believe in you and the power of your might: when I am in need, I will look to the hill from whence cometh my help, all of my help comes from the Lord who made heaven and earth. You will not suffer thy foot to be moved. You that keepeth thee will not slumber. Behold, you that keepeth Israel shall neither slumber nor sleep. LORD, you are my keeper! LORD, you are my shade upon your right hand.

Lord, here am I. I know that if I ask, then it shall be given; if I seek, then I shall find, and if I knock, then the door will be opened. It is true that we have not because we ask not. Though faith has made me whole, I am healed by your stripes. I thank you Lord that whatever I ask in Jesus' name, it shall be given to me. I know you are able to do anything but fail. Lord I thank you that you will increase my faith. In Jesus' name, amen!

Prayer for Healing and Strength

Let us pray to be healed and strengthened through our pain.

Gracious and eternal God, the one who rules heaven and earth. The one who sent His only son to Calvary for us that we may have the right to the tree of life. Here I am before you, oh God, asking for mercy and grace. Asking that you will not pass me by, asking that you hear my humble cry.

Lord, I need you like never before. I need you on my job, in my home, in the church house, in the White House, and in my neighborhood. I plead your blood, Jesus, over every door post, church, home, property, land and even the school house and buses.

God, bind our mind to the will of God. Help us to bind up the strongman and every strong hold that has us in bondage. I come against sickness and disease, every type of cancer, high blood pressure, heart problems, diabetes, lupus, and sickle cell.

Jesus, you were wounded for my transgressions, bruised for my iniquities, but by your stripes, I am healed! You bore my grief and carried my sorrow. I have no one but you God.

Some need you for one thing, and others for another. I am standing in the gap for them, asking that you will hear our collective cry and deliver us from all our troubles. You said to ask and it shall be given, seek and ye shall find, knock and the doors will open. You said that our Heavenly Father will take care of us, that whoever will call upon His name, they shall be saved.

You came that we may have life and have it more abundantly. You said to cast our cares on you because you care. You said to have faith as a mustard seed. You said what better friend is one who would lay down his life for one. When the righteous cry out, the Lord heareth. You said that we come boldly to the throne of grace that we may obtain mercy and find grace to help in times of need. You have promised that although weapons of this type of warfare are not carnal, they are mighty through God, and will pull down every stronghold. These weapons will cast down every imagination and every high thing that exalt itself against the knowledge of God. These weapons will also bring into captivity every thought to the obedience of Christ, and having in readiness to revenge all disobedience when our obedience is full.

Lord, you have given us our hands to war with. Now, Lord, give us the strength to endure and to keep the whole amour on. Lord, protect our children as they go back to school: keep them from gangs, peer pressure, pride, rebellion, and the lustful desires of spirits that seek to entangle them. Empower them to make great decisions and help to pass every assignment and test that they will receive. I pray that you will give teachers patience, meekness, and gentleness to help them along the way. God, restore all relationships that you have joined: marriages, mothers and daughters, fathers and sons, daughters and sons, sisters and brothers, fathers and daughters, in laws and outlaws, pastors and preachers to their members.

God, have your way, in Jesus' name Amen!

Prayer for God's Presence

When we are in pain, it is imperative that we seek God. This is a prayer to ask Him to make His face plain to us as we are going through trials and tribulation.

Thank you God for this day, for this is the day that you have made and I will rejoice in it. Thank you God for allowing me to have access to you and ask for whatever it is I need. Knowing that you are God alone and there is no other, I am grateful to have a father I can call on to hear my cry and who will answer me.

I come humbly asking you to forgive my sins. God, please restore to me the power of the Holy Ghost. Do not take your presence away from me. Create in me a clean heart and renew a right spirit in me. I know that He that dwell in the secret place of the most high shall abide in the shadow of the almighty. I ask that you hide me in your secret pavilion. I need your glory, I want to feel you glory, I need your power and I need your presence. Without you, I am nothing and can do nothing. Breath on me, wash me, purge me and make me over. Place me back on the potter's wheel and make me again. Mold me and shape me until I look like you.

If I dwell in you, you will dwell in me. If I delight myself in you, you will give me the desires of my heart. Thank you God that your love is everlasting and you are a forgiving God. God, give us an ear to hear what the spirit of the Lord is saying. I want more of you, to be led to do your will. Amen!

> *Psalms 51:11 Cast me not away from thy presence; and take not thy holy spirit from me. Restore unto me the joy of thy salvation; and uphold me with thy free spirit.*

Prayer of Relief
Psalms 63

1To the chief Musician upon Shoshannim, A Psalm of David. Save me, O God; for the waters are come in unto my soul.

2I sink in deep mire, where there is no standing: I am come into deep waters, where the floods overflow me.

3I am weary of my crying: my throat is dried: mine eyes fail while I wait for my God.

4They that hate me without a cause are more than the hairs of mine head: they that would destroy me, being mine enemies wrongfully, are mighty: then I restored that which I took not away.

5O God, thou knowest my foolishness; and my sins are not hid from thee.

6Let not them that wait on thee, O Lord GOD of hosts, be ashamed for my sake: let not those that seek thee be confounded for my sake, O God of Israel.

7Because for thy sake I have borne reproach; shame hath covered my face.

8I am become a stranger unto my brethren, and an alien unto my mother's children.

9For the zeal of thine house hath eaten me up; and the reproaches of them that reproached thee are fallen upon me.

10   When I wept, and chastened my soul with fasting, that was to my reproach. 11 I made sackcloth also my garment; and I became a proverb to them.

12   They that sit in the gate speak against me; and I was the song of the drunkards.

13   But as for me, my prayer is unto thee, O LORD, in an acceptable time: O God, in the multitude of thy mercy hear me, in the truth of thy salvation.

14   Deliver me out of the mire, and let me not sink: let me be delivered from them that hate me, and out of the deep waters.

15   Let not the water flood overflow me, neither let the deep swallow me up, and let not the pit shut her mouth upon me.

16   Hear me, O LORD; for thy loving kindness is good: turn unto me according to the multitude of thy tender mercies.

17   And hide not thy face from thy servant; for I am in trouble: hear me speedily. 18 Draw nigh unto my soul, and redeem it: deliver me because of mine enemies.

19   Thou hast known my reproach, and my shame, and my dishonor: mine adversaries are all before thee.

20   Reproach hath broken my heart; and I am full of heaviness: and I looked for some to take pity, but there was none; and for comforters, but I found none.

21   They gave me also gall for my meat; and in my thirst they gave me vinegar to drink. 22 Let their table become a snare before them: and that which should have been for their

welfare, let it become a trap.

23 Let their eyes be darkened, that they see not; and make their loins continually to shake. 24 Pour out thine indignation upon them, and let thy wrathful anger take hold of them.

25   Let their habitation be desolate; and let none dwell in their tents.

26   For they persecute him whom thou hast smitten; and they talk to the grief of those whom thou hast wounded.

27   Add iniquity unto their iniquity: and let them not come into thy righteousness.

28   Let them be blotted out of the book of the living, and not be written with the righteous. 29 But I am poor and sorrowful: let thy salvation, O God, set me up on high.

30   I will praise the name of God with a song, and will magnify him with thanksgiving.

31   This also shall please the LORD better than an ox or bullock that hath horns and hoofs. 32 The humble shall see this, and be glad: and your heart shall live that seek God.

33   For the LORD heareth the poor, and despiseth not his prisoners.

34   Let the heaven and earth praise him, the seas, and everything that moveth therein.

35   For God will save Zion, and will build the cities of Judah: that they may dwell there, and have it in possession.

36   The seed also of his servants shall inherit it: and they that love his name shall dwell therein.

Prayer for Provision

This is a prayer for use when one feels lack. God gave us dominion over this earth; whatever you need, it is here and it is yours. But you must ask for it!

Our Father which art in heaven, hollowed be thy name. Thy kingdom come thy will be done. Give us this day our daily bread. Lord forgive us of our trespasses and forgive those who trespass against us. (The Lord's Prayer)

Lord, we know that you are peace in the midst of any storm, you are a bridge over troubled waters, you are a mind regulator, lawyer in the court room and doctor in the hospital. You are a provider and a pro-visionary. God, you are a way out of no way. You are a strong tower and our refuge.

Lord, have mercy on us. God, hear and answer this prayer. Bless your people on their jobs, cancel every debt, give promotions and increase. I declare and decree everything I have prayed shall be in Jesus' name. Lord cancel every plot and plan that the devil has sent out. In the name of Jesus, I command you Satan to render powerless and loose your hold off the people of God.

No weapon formed against us shall prosper and every tongue that rise against us, God shall condemn. Lord, keep your arms of protection around our children. Protect them from peer pressure and violence. I plead the blood of Jesus all around them right now.

Lord, direct our paths and help us to be godly women and men. All that you have called us to be, stir up the gift that you have given us so that our gift will make room for us. Lord, I just want to serve you and be a blessing to your people that they may see the glory of God through me.

I love you God and thank you. Amen.

Prayer to Break Strongholds

Dear Heavenly Father, holy is thy name. For you are holy. I just want to say thank you for who you are. You have been so good to us. I cannot began to count all the things you have done in our lives. I can praise your name! I worship you from the depths of my soul. I am standing in the gap for my sisters and brothers. Lord, have mercy on us. We need you to save those who are lost, heal those who are hurting in their hearts: hurting because of past relationships, hurting because they have lost a loved one or someone left them.

God, deliver your people from the ways of the world, deliver us from temptation, deliver us from self, deliver us and set the captives free!

Lord, please give us a renewed spirit and transformed mind and your understanding. Lord, I pray for peace that surpasses all understanding.

Make our enemies our footstools. Bless our going out and our coming in. Bless us in the city and in the field. I bind the works of the enemy. I cancel every plot and plan, I come against every spirit of fear and command you to render them powerless, in Jesus' name.

Break every generational curse and every soul tie. Loose your hold, you devil! I send angels to encamp around our homes, properties, ministries, jobs, schools, and vehicles. I plead the blood of JESUS over all the children and bind the spirit of peer pressure and intimidation.

Every strong hold will be brought down in Jesus' name, casting down every imagination that exalt itself against the knowledge of Christ.

God, I thank you right now that every crooked road shall be made straight and every lie shall be revealed. Every tongue that rises up against us, JESUS you shall condemn. No weapon formed against us shall prosper and it is in Jesus' name I pray. Amen.

Prayer for Understanding

Life is full of opportunities to misunderstand people. It is why we must be patient and kind in giving people the benefit of the doubt when we perceive harm in what they say and/or do. Do not be so quick to judge people; think things through and give them a second chance to make a first impression. **James 1:19 "Wherefore, my beloved brethren, let every man be swift to hear, slow to speak, slow to wrath."**

Dear Heavenly Father, I come to you to ask for forgiveness of anything that I may have said, thought or done that caused injury or pain to another. Lord, please show me what I can do to communicate better to the people who surrounds me. Lord, you have given me the power to speak life or death in any situation. Today Lord I ask that you will move in me and show me who you have called me to be. Lord, touch those who I have to work with, or come in contact with on a daily basis, and let the light that shines in me bless them.

Because of who I am in you Lord some people do not understand or do not want to see the goodness of you have placed in me . I know Lord that your light shines in me and that I am a chosen vessel that you have brought out of darkness into the marvelous light. I am not perfect, but every day I am striving for perfection. If I offended anyone Lord please forgive me and I pray they will forgive me also.

Lord, you created me differently from any other and I thank you for that uniqueness. I thank you that I am the apple of your eye. I thank you that I am fearfully and wonderfully made. Lord, I thank you that you decided to call me friend. I thank you that despite of all my flaws, and sometimes I may be wrong, Lord you still love me.

I pray for those who cannot understand me, and ask that you give me understanding to walk in who you have called me to be. Amen.

Psalm 119:104 "Through thy precepts I get understanding: therefore I hate every false way. Thy word is a lamp unto my feet, and a light unto my path. I have sworn, and I will perform it, that I will keep thy righteous judgments."

A Prayer of Thanks

Being grateful during pain is a sure way to frustrate the enemy's plans and fortify your mind against thoughts that would weaken your resolve to get through it. Pray this prayer to convey gratefulness and thanks to the Almighty Father.

Father, Jesus, Savior, Jehovah, Elshada, Elohim, Adona, Prince of Peace, the bright and Morning Star, Alpha and Omega.

Thank you for allowing us to see another day. Thank you for who you are. Thank you for watching over us all night long. Thank you for the people in our lives and our family. Thank you for being for being faithful. Thank you for your goodness toward us. Thank you for your mercy and love. Thank you for looking beyond our faults and supplying all our needs.

Thank you because you said if we forgive, you will forgive us. Thank you for washing us clean with your blood. Thank you because you called us friend. Thank you for interceding on our behalf. Thank you for answering prayer. Thank you for guidance. Thank you for giving.

Thank you for protection. Thank you for patience. Thank you for providing. Thank you for the promotion and the promise. Thank you for peace. Thank you for prosperity.

Thank you for dying on the cross so that we may have life everlasting. Thank you for healing. Thank you for heaven. Thank you for strength, stability, and salvation. Thank you for deliverance, direction, and destination.

Thank you for separation. Thank you for restoration and rejuvenation and motivation. Thank you for your word. Thank you for all you have done, are doing and will do in Jesus' name.

Amen.

Prayer for the Pain

Praying helps to focus our minds on the good things in life, the blessings God has allowed to rain down on us. Here is a prayer to help you in the midst of the pain.

Father, in the name of Jesus, I come boldly to the throne of grace to obtain mercy and grace in the time of need. You are the king of king, Lord of Lords, you are the way, the truth, and the life. You never sleep nor slumber, but you have the whole world in your hand.

Now God I know that you hear your people crying out, pleading, and even begging for help. Lord, we need you more now than ever. We cannot do nothing without you, and we cannot do anything until you come. Come Lord to our homes, the hospitals, to the jobs, the church and even in the school house. Make your presence known, for you will fight our battle and vengeance is yours. You said to stand after we have done all we can do. You told us to call upon your name, and you will hear and deliver us from all of our troubles.

I was young, but now I am old; I have never seen the righteous forsaken nor God's seed begging for bread. The effectual fervent prayers of the righteous availeth much. You shall supply all of our needs according to your riches in glory. Fix what is broken, heal what is hurting, mend what is wounded. I know you can heal this land, for you were wounded for our transgressions, bruised for our inequities and the chastisement of peace was upon you, and by your stripes we are healed.

No weapon formed against us shall prosper, every tongue that rise against us, you shall condemn. We are a chosen generation, a royal priesthood, who shall shew forth the praises of your people, who were once in darkness, but are now in light. Lord, I know all things work together for the good of them who love the Lord and are called according to your purpose. Lord, help us to walk in unity and not destruction, peace and not war, humility and not pride, love and not hate, understanding and not ignorance, on one accord and without division.

Help us to be a better people that we may become more like you. "For if my people who are called by my name shall humble themselves, turn from their wicked ways, seek My face, pray, then shall I forgive their sins, answer their prayers and heal the land." These are your words God. I am praying for miracles and standing in the gap for healing in this land, peace, unity and love. Lord, forgive us of anything we may have said, thought, or done that was not pleasing in your sight. In Jesus' name,

Amen.

Prayer for the Family

Father, in the name of Jesus, we thank you that you are King of kings, Lord of lords, and that you are in control of every situation. Thank you that you will never fail us, and what you promised you will perform.

Lord, forgive us of our sins, and forgive those who trespass against us. Help us to love one another. Create in us a clean heart and renew a right spirit in us. Change our minds so we can think right, change our hearts so we may love right, change our tongues so we may talk right.

Lord we need you right now. We cannot live without you, or have our own being without you.

Remove every hindrance, distraction, confusion, discord and distinction between all family members. Restore this family with love, peace, joy, faith and gentleness, meekness, and long suffering. God we plead the blood of Jesus over them right now. We bind up every strong hold, generational curse, Python spirit, Absolom spirit, Jezebel spirit, deaf and dumb spirit in the name of Jesus. Jesus, send them back to the pits of hell from which they come and allow them never to return again.

Lord, heal the hurt and pain, mend brokenness, lift every weight and sin that so easily beset us.

We thank you for your tender mercy and grace that cover us daily. We thank you that you are a present help in the time of need. Our refuge and strength, our light and salvation. Thank you Lord for your unconditional love.

In Jesus' name, amen!

Prayer for Healing Wounds

God, I want to thank you for being the Lord of my life, and adopting me as your child. I now have access to the Father and I do not have to wait on a high priest because you are that high priest.

God, I thank you that you are a very present help in times of trouble. I thank you that you are my peace in the midst of a storm, you are a bridge over trouble waters, you are a dwelling place, that you will hide me in your secret tabernacle. Lord, that you hear my cry in the midnight hour and you come to my rescue. Lord, when the weight is too much to bear, you are always present.

When I am hurting, you are there to mend the wounds. I thank you that you were wounded for my transgressions and bruised for my iniquities. Thank you for carrying the chastisement of peace upon your shoulders, and with your stripes I am healed of all the pain, anger, bitterness, unforgiveness, soul ties, and every other hurt.

Thank you, Lord for your blood; the blood of Jesus heals the hurt, it delivers, it saves, it will never lose its power.

In Jesus' name, amen!

ABOUT THE AUTHOR

Evangelist Stephanie Berry Davenport is the daughter of Lillie Cooper and Michael Lovelace. She was born on March 22, 1971. She resides in West Point, GA., where she was raised by her grandmother, Gussie M. Wilson. Stephanie graduated from Troup High School in 1989. She attended West Georgia Tech for Marketing, Kerr Business College for Accounting and Bethlehem Theological Christian Academy where she received her certificate. She accepted her calling on October 12, 2008, and was licensed to preach the gospel and proposed to on the same night. She went on to marry Mr. Alvin Davenport on June 13, 2009. Stephanie has a wonderful daughter by the name of Serita Harvey.

Evangelist Davenport received her Associates Degree in Biblical Arts from Leverett Hill School of Theology by Cornerstone Schools. She is currently attending college to receive her Bachelor's Degree. Evangelist Davenport serves as a faithful member under the leadership of Dr. W.T. Edmondson at Bethlehem Baptist Church located in West Point, GA. Evangelist Davenport is a preacher , prophet of God and published author. Her ministry is to heal hurting men and women. On April 27, 2015, 30 Days to Heal Your Soul was released to the public. Stephanie knows God has a calling on her life and she wants to share His love and His message to everyone she meets.

"The spirit of the Lord is upon me, because he has anointed me to preach the Gospel to the poor, he hath sent me to heal the broken hearted, to preach deliverance to the captives, and recovering the sight to the blind, to set at liberty them that are bruised, t o preach the acceptable year of the Lord!"

Made in the USA
Charleston, SC
28 June 2016